SELF-LOVE FOR WOMEN

How to love yourself when you've been emotionally hurt,
taken for granted, and abused

Volume One

A l e x a n d e r   M c E w e n

Dedicated to my mother Patrice

Having you as my mother has been one of the greatest blessings in my life. I love you.

TABLE OF CONTENTS

INTRODUCTION

I was taught as a child by my mother that the heart takes the longest to heal. Before meeting my father, she experienced heartbreak. She had met this other man during her sophomore year in high school. Years into the relationship, she was convinced that this would be the person she would marry. However, as time went on, she started to notice changes in his behavior. My mother began to feel in her heart that something was not right. Doubts flooded her mind as if they were a daily ritual.

She started to see less of him but refused to pay attention to the signs. Until one day, as she was going to the movies, she saw him holding hands with another woman. My mother found out that they had just gotten married. To make matters worse, the woman was also pregnant with his child.

It took my mother years to get over him. She was afraid to take anyone seriously after that experience. Eventually, she did, and that man happened to be my father.

Upon hearing that story, I remember thinking it would be wonderful to speed up the healing process. If there was any way to uplift the soul when the heart had been broken, I was interested. The mind is known for telling lies when we have a habit of not feeding it the truth. We start to believe it's our fault regardless of whether we did our best. But, no matter the pain, you still deserve to have joy in your life. This book was written to repair your heart with love, removing all thoughts of not feeling worthy and replacing them with empowerment. The sooner you are healed, the faster you can move forward with your life.

Let us revisit any painful memory that's on your mind and write a new interpretation. This will take honesty and the ability to see things as they are and not make them worse. It will take patience, reflecting on any experience that may perhaps be the roadblock in your life. Lastly, it will take self-love, having the healthy relationship with yourself that your body deserves. Allow this book to remind you of how much you have to offer.

Self-Love For Women

CHAPTER ONE

HEARTBREAK TRANSFORMATION

Her name is Kayla. While traveling to different countries, she met someone in India. He happened to be everything she looked for in a man, charming, sense of humor, and a warm spirit. They had a strong connection and eventually began traveling together. For six months, they stayed in some of the most beautiful places in India. With so much time spent together, they ended up falling in love.

Kayla was living on cloud nine. Everything seemed to be happening so fast. It wasn't until they got back to their homes that she discovered something. She was losing herself. Her entire life became all about what he wanted, and her desires were never acknowledged. As time went on, Kayla began to get jealous and insecure. She found herself taking things more personally and getting upset often. Finally, she decided to end the relationship.

The breakup was painful, as you can imagine. There were a lot of tears shed on many nights. Wanting to cheer her up, Kayla's sister insisted that they get away together for a vacation. Hesitant at first, she reluctantly agreed.

By getting away from everything, she learned an invaluable lesson: You don't have to lose yourself when you fall in love. Just because you are in a relationship doesn't mean that you ARE the relationship. You are still your own person with wants, desires, and needs. You may still have ambitions about other things you want to do in life too. While compromises will be made in a relationship, the ones that succeed are the ones who both want each other's happiness. She made everything that he did more important than what she wanted.

Jessica has a similar story. When she broke up with her boyfriend, she felt lost. They had been together for four years and had their whole future planned out. After the relationship ended, she decided to be more open to invites from friends. She found herself saying yes to almost every opportunity. Her productivity at work increased, which led to a promotion. Physically she became stronger from going to the gym. She even trained and ran for the New York City Marathon. Jessica found this experience to be the most liberating. She was finally able to be alone with her thoughts and feel empowered.

I'm not sure where you find yourself as you're reading this. Whether you ended a relationship recently or someone ended it with you, your life will and must go on. All of our experiences can empower us when used wisely. I heard about another woman who went through a heartbreak but shortly thereafter met her special man. She's quoted as saying, "Thank God that the guy broke up with me because otherwise, I would've never met the love of my life." Take this time to focus on the areas about yourself that have been neglected. Now is the opportunity to love them like never before. I'm sure the little girl in you had a vision of how she was going to live her life when she grew up. Be childlike and revisit those moments.

I want to end this chapter with a quote I came across online that I thought was powerful from Mind Journal. "Be thankful for every heartbreak, for they were planned. They come into your life just to reveal another layer of yourself to you and then leave. Their purpose is to shake you up, tear apart your ego a little bit, show you your obstacles and addictions, break your heart open so new light can get in, make you so desperate and out of control that you have to transform your life. And you do." You are being transformed; embrace it.

Self-Love For Women

CHAPTER TWO

FORGIVENESS

M adison's father died when she was 6 years old in a car accident. Her mother began dating a man sometime afterward who happened to be a drug addict. He managed to manipulate and steal all of the settlement money from her father's death. The next man Madison's mother dated was physically abusive. Fearing that no one else would love her, she stayed with him anyway.

When Madison was 11 years old, he then began to sexually abuse her. She told her mother immediately, hoping that would put an end to it. Instead, her mother began beating her regularly and forced her to go along with it. The abuse went on for years affecting not only Madison but her siblings too. It only stopped when the man broke her mother's neck, almost paralyzing her. While in the hospital, Child Protective Services were called and found out about the abuse. They gave Madison's mother an ultimatum. She would have to leave this man once and for all to keep her children.

Madison was relieved. After years of being abused, she was going to finally be able to live a normal life with her mother, only to find out her mother chose to marry him while lying in the hospital bed. Madison and her siblings were then sent to live with her grandparents.

For years she hated her mother. She could never understand why her mother would let her go through so much pain. Her childhood was miserable, and she blamed her for every part of it. Then one night, when Madison was alone at home, she got on her knees and began to pray. The bitterness she had towards her mother was having a negative impact on her life. Deep down inside, she knew something needed to change. She asked God to see her mother as he sees her. She wanted to be able to love her mother unconditionally despite the pain. When Madison was done with her prayer, she felt like the universe was lifted off her shoulders.

Today, she now has a loving relationship with her mother. Her perspective has forever changed whenever she reflects on the past. She sees a woman who was emotionally torn apart after the loss of her husband and father of her kids.

Learning to forgive may be one of the hardest challenges in life. When someone does us wrong, it's usually taken personally.

While many times it can be uncomfortable to do, forgiveness is needed on your journey of self-love. Some people may not even care whether you forgive them or not. Always remember you're doing it so that you can be free. This next woman had unbelievable compassion to do what she did.

Manchester Arena Suicide Bombing

It was May 22, 2017; Lauren had already gone to bed but was awakened by her daughter. She told her that her brother had gone to a concert and there was an explosion at the arena. His friends were looking for him all night and wanted to see if he had contacted her. Startled by her daughter's words, she ran downstairs, where she found her husband watching the news. He did his best to cheer her up and not let her think the worst. The investigation was still in process, so there was still a chance that he may be alive.

As you can imagine, Lauren and her family were unable to sleep that night. They continued to watch the news for the next 24 hours, but she already knew the truth. Her son was murdered in the suicide bombing. Shortly thereafter, she got a phone call, and it was confirmed.

Losing your child is a parent's worst nightmare. No one ever dreams of having to bury their son or daughter. Since it wasn't a surprise to Lauren when it was confirmed, she put all her focus on being there for her other kids. A few days after the tragedy, she saw a picture of the bomber for the first time in a newspaper. He was only 22 years old. She couldn't believe that someone so young would ever think of doing such a horrific act. There was still more life for him to live as well, just as the others.

Weeks went by, and Lauren could not forget the image. She finally made the hardest decision she's ever had to make in her life. She decided to forgive him. Lauren knew that living with anger and hate would never bring her son back. It would only cause her to view the world as cruel. She was one of the first to go public about her forgiveness towards the man. Many people disagreed with her decision, and she got trolled harshly on social media. Their actions had no effect on her. She wanted to be an example for her children about forgiveness. Her son was a kind-hearted young man. She knew in her heart that he would want her to carry on living life with love.

The Manchester bombing inspired Lauren to try and understand why people do what they do. She decided to get her Master's degree in counterterrorism. She quickly learned that the real criminals are not the ones who commit these acts but the ones who manipulate them into doing so. These people grow up believing what they are doing is right.

Lauren's story may be unimaginable to many of you. She's an example of using whatever life offers her in a positive way. Indian yoga guru and author Sadhguru said a powerful quote when asked about forgiveness. "Anger, resentment, and hatred are all poisons that you take and expect someone else to die. Life doesn't work like that. You drink poison, you die. It's a very fair life."

Forgiveness does not mean accepting intolerable behavior. There are some people who you will have to continue keeping your distance from after forgiving. These are the people who will always cause harm to your life because of toxicity. No matter the chances given, they will find ways to abuse the relationship. However, I do believe the heart grows larger with compassion when you're able to let things go. Painful memories do nothing for the body except cause stress and other illnesses. Releasing anything that is hurting you is spiritual medicine for the soul.

Forgive yourself. We often hear these words from everywhere but rarely do we live by them. Do you ever notice how easy it is to tell someone to forgive themselves, but how hard it is for us to do the same?

My mother is the most loving woman in my eyes and has apologized to me many times about events in the past. Despite the acknowledgment and appreciation I have for her she too would have her moments of feeling down. One day I came home from work, and she was crying about something she had said to me out of anger years ago. Her mind was making her feel bad about the situation as if it just happened. Even though it never crossed my mind, it consumed her. I told her that she was forgiven then and that it was time to forgive herself. It was important that she no longer lived her life reflecting on imperfections. We all have them.

My mother finally did forgive herself and felt free. When thoughts enter her mind now she no longer lets them get the best of her.

Another similar experience happened to a friend of mine. She made a mistake and betrayed the trust of someone in her life. Her friend refused to confide in her anymore, which brought her to tears. Each time my friend would think about it, she felt miserable. She began judging herself harshly, forgetting anything good she did in the relationship.

Many times in life, we make mistakes and beat ourselves up for them. Whether it was something that we said or did we never let it go. It's important to understand that our actions will never be perfect. There will be moments when we are not at our best. Instead of beating ourselves up, we need to ask for forgiveness from those we hurt, but most importantly, we need to forgive ourselves.

It was the year 1982, and Brianna was only 13 years old. She had been having a difficult childhood up to that point. Things were not the greatest at home, and she was bullied often in school. The only thing that Brianna looked forward to doing was playing sports. That was her escape from the misery she faced in her everyday life. She tried out for track and field and made the javelin team.

Brianna made up her mind that she was going to win a medal for this event. At her first meet, when it was her turn, she ran and threw the javelin with all her strength. It seemed to be going straight at first but then it started to sway towards the right. One of her friends had volunteered to mark the distance, but unfortunately, she was distracted. In the blink of an eye, the javelin struck her in the head and immediately brought her to the ground. Blood began to gush from her head like a running faucet. Brianna fell to her knees in horror. She thought for sure she blinded her friend.

Later her mother took her to the hospital to make sure her friend was okay. However, she was faced with the most devastating news, her friend had died from the event. Brianna went into shock. She couldn't believe what she was hearing. Just the other day, she had been spending time with her friend, and now she was dead. When the police interviewed everyone, the verdict was "Death by Misadventure." This meant that everything could've been prevented, and the school took full responsibility.

It would be years later before Brianna discovered that. She spent most of her life blaming herself for what she had done. While her family was there for her at home, she could never escape the guilt. She began to write to her friend daily to ease the pain. That was her only way to begin healing herself.

She later found out that her friend's parents never blamed her for the incident. They knew that she would never purposely harm their daughter. Nevertheless, Brianna continued to struggle with forgiving herself. She never married or had any children. It wasn't until years later, when she signed up for Cognitive Behavioral Therapy, that she began to shift her thinking. She then knew she had to finally forgive herself.

Brianna began to look back at that moment with a new perspective. She realized that she was an innocent young girl who was only trying to play sports. Brianna never got into trouble at school and always got decent grades. It was that one moment that made her view her life as a failure. She then decided to reclaim her life. She revisited the memory and began telling herself a more compassionate story, that she never meant to hurt her friend. She now does coaching and training workshops that focus on transforming mental well-being.

We must be surrounded by people that remind us of our true nature. Our minds are powerful, as you know. The fastest way to get over anything in your life is by revisiting it and giving it a different meaning. We're no longer going to run away from the pain; we're going to face it head-on reminding it that we are in control. So right now, as you're reading, I want you to think about what's hurting you at this moment. What is something that you're having difficulty letting go of?

Next, I want you to go in front of a mirror and say with conviction, "I forgive you. The choices I made in the past were based on my level of thought then, not now." I want you to keep saying it repeatedly until you begin to believe it. The beautiful woman you're looking at in this mirror is all you got. She deserves to be loved, held, and forgiven unconditionally no matter what. Only when you can begin to smile at yourself, do I want you to walk away from the mirror.

Allow today to be the beginning of a new journey for your life. Letting go of old destructive habits and replacing them with empowering ones. Revisit this chapter as many times as needed. The more you flood your mind with the truth, it becomes easier to let go of the pain. Everyone needs a warm reminder that they are not their decisions. The sooner that's understood, the faster you'll be able to move forward with your life. Some people will attempt to hold grudges against you. No matter the apology, they will not accept it. You will never have control over their decision, but you will always have control over forgiving yourself.

CHAPTER THREE

TEACH PEOPLE
HOW TO TREAT YOU

If you don't teach people how to treat you, they will never know. This actually makes me think of a powerful scene from the movie *The Color Purple*. If you haven't seen it, I highly recommend it. It stars Whoopi Goldberg, Danny Glover, and was Oprah Winfrey's first acting role. In the scene, a woman compliments how clean Oprah's kids are and asks them if they would like to be her maid. Oprah immediately responded, "Hell no." This made a gentleman nearby come over and actually slap her. Without hesitation, Oprah's character balled up her fist and knocked him to the ground.

Now, this chapter is not written for you to go beat up everyone who has done you wrong. It's to encourage you to begin having boundaries of what you're willing to accept. The worst thing you can do is to assume everyone will treat you the way you want without your help.

I want you to picture this. Whenever you meet someone new, you both are entering a class taught by one another. When paying attention in this class, you will learn all about this person. Their likes, dislikes, and what makes them feel appreciated. While not all will pass this class, and some will ignore the lessons, there will definitely be others who are eager to learn if you verbally share with them.

I'm sure you've heard the phrase "all men are the same" or "all women are the same." I have never believed that for a moment. What I do believe is that some people want to be in your class and others don't. You are the only one that can make that distinction. So, no matter the pain you're feeling at this time, your frustration should not be applied to everyone.

Acknowledge The Pattern

Danielle grew up in an abusive household. While her parents never put their hands on her, both of them were verbally and physically abusive towards one another. Whenever there was the slightest disagreement, words were used to attack. Shortly afterward fists were thrown from both sides. This was a vicious cycle. Neither one ever bothered listening to what the other had to say. They were both too busy in reactive mode and ready to fight.

Eventually, the marriage ended, but Danielle never forgot those memories.

When she came of age, she began to date as well. Danielle quickly discovered she was repeating her parents' behavior. When she didn't get her way, she would scream and put her hands on her partner. The both of them would fight weekly until the relationship ended. These altercations went on for years.

Danielle could not understand why she was attracting these types of relationships. It wasn't until she became close to someone who had high self-esteem that she discovered the problem. The friend pointed out some potential changes that needed to be made and challenged her to answer questions about herself.

Danielle knew the type of person that she wanted and decided to begin with herself. She began to become more compassionate. Her language on how she spoke to herself changed for the better. She developed patience and became a great listener with friends. Danielle became the woman that a healthy partner would want to be with, and in return, successfully found the same qualities in her next relationship.

You can always tell a lot about a person from how they respond when angry. Everyone can be nice when things are going their way. It's important to observe them when facing adversity. So now I challenge you to ask the following questions to yourself. How do you respond when you're angry? Do you lose control? Do you begin cursing the other person out? Most importantly, do you want your partner to be the same towards you? We all have our moments when we are not our best selves. However, acknowledging that is not an excuse to become disrespectful. Every day you should strive to be respectful towards one another if you want the same. It's also essential to have people that can make us aware of things in the relationship that we're unable to see.

Motivational speaker Les Brown says, "You can't see the picture when you're in the frame." Love is blind. When you're in a relationship, there will always be blind spots. Whether that be areas that you're not able to see because you're in it or qualities that you see but refuse to acknowledge. It's important to seek advice from those that are genuine and will tell you the truth with no hidden agenda. It's better to have your feelings hurt from the truth than to have your heart broken from lies.

I remember a woman I met at Wharton High School in Tampa, Florida. She had to have been one of the sweetest people I had met at that time. Every day she had a smile on her face and such a positive way of viewing life.

What also stood out to me about this woman was that she was choosing to be celibate. In high school, where hormones can be almost uncontrollable, you have this amazing woman deciding not to have sex until marriage. She went through a phase of not finding what she wanted from a relationship. Everyone she spoke to only wanted one thing. I'm sure each experience caused her pain.

Nevertheless, she refused to rearrange her values to make someone else feel good. Eventually, she ended up meeting the man of her dreams. Someone who respected her wishes and was willing to wait. Today, they have been married for close to ten years and have two beautiful kids.

Sometimes it may feel like the world is pushing you to change your values. You're looking left and right for your ideal partner but are continuously disappointed. I'm here to tell you to not throw in the towel. These individuals always seem to appear in our lives when we least expect them.

Self-Love For Women

CHAPTER FOUR

KNOWING WHEN
TO LET SOMEONE GO

This is a difficult chapter to write for many reasons. No one dreams of ending their relationship when they begin it, especially when so much time has been invested. When you bring kids into the picture, it can be more of a challenge. Know that these words are written with the utmost empathy. I understand that everyone's situation is different. Therefore this is about being brutally honest with yourself. I'm going to share two stories with you before going more in-depth. I want to do my best to touch on everything before you get to the next chapter.

She had just won the academy award for best actress. In her acceptance speech, she thanked her husband for his support. He had tears in his eyes as she mentioned his name. She was beyond thankful for this moment. Halle Berry felt like she had everything she ever wanted. Shortly thereafter, she found out a magazine had posted a story about her husband. It appeared that he had been seeing another woman. She didn't believe it for one second and decided she was going to sue them. But, a week later her husband finally told her it was true.

Halle was deeply hurt but was determined to still get through it. Then later, she found out there were many other women. She did her best to move forward but eventually decided to end the marriage. Halle knew she couldn't trust him again and didn't want to live that way.

This other artist was also cheated on. She ended up using her music as a way to cope with the pain. She believed that he was not the worst of what he had done. In many ways, it was therapy for her and her husband. He also recorded music on his own to vent as well. It was painful for both of them, but they decided to commit themselves to making their marriage work. The artists I'm referring to are Beyoncé and her husband, Jay-Z.

What's important to remember is that there is no universal way to approach this kind of situation. Everyone is different. This is where you have to be honest with yourself more than ever. When you go through these unfortunate events, your friends or family will do everything to cheer you up. That is what they are there for. Those who are closest to you want to see you happy.

They will then give you their advice on what you should do. Some will say attempt to work it out for the kids. You don't want them to be in a broken family. Others will say to leave your partner because they obviously have no respect for you, and that is why they cheated.

The woman who makes the final decision is yourself. If you are someone that believes you can eventually get through this and is someone who has a partner that is just as committed to making it work as you are, be willing to search for what went wrong so that it doesn't happen again. Know that it will be a tough road ahead but still be determined to make it work. You need to be willing to perhaps get counsel or pray with your partner. Be willing to accept their apology and move forward. You must be determined to build up the trust again and let the past go. If you're willing to do this and your partner is sincere in their apology, then I encourage you to do your best to make it work.

On the other hand, if you are someone who knows you will never be able to let this go and that in your heart, you will not be able to trust this person again, you have to be strong enough to walk away . Otherwise, you will always dwell on the fact that they cheated on you and will probably bring this up during each argument moving forward. If you feel that you will always be insecure and unhappy because of it, then I encourage you to let them go. There is no need to go forward with that person if you know you're going to be miserable.

You Can't Make Someone Be The One, They Just Are

Have you ever met someone that had everything you looked for physically? They were the right height, had a nice smile, and had a great physique? I'm sure you have; we all have. We see these people every day, depending on where we live. The common mistake that many of us make is that we try to make someone be the one. We do our best to mold them into the ideal person we want them to be. But more often than not, we are unsuccessful in our molding. It doesn't always last.

Becoming the *one* is a mutual desire. It's when both people are on the same page about what they want in their lives. It's when needs are happily met because you both can't picture life without one another. It's when the soul meets its counterpart and combines creating something special. While it may be a challenge due to past experiences, I promise you your faith will attract them into your life. In the meantime, you have to be honest with yourself no matter how amazing this person looks.

There are some people who believe that you cannot have both. You can either have someone who looks good or treats you well. I believe that you can have both and know many people that have the whole package. Make no mistake that they are not perfect either. However, their personalities complement their looks. They are genuine people. You have to do your part and stay mentally grounded in your search.

You Can't Force Chemistry

Just like you can't make someone be the one, you also cannot force chemistry. Many times when you first meet someone of interest, you'll find yourself doing things to keep their attention. Charm, humor, and respect are all displayed at the highest level. While appearances are known to arouse the eyes, you cannot force a genuine connection. Falling in love with looks alone can lead to despair, but falling in love with who they are will lead to happiness. If you happen to be single, these are the lessons to remember the next time you meet someone. It can save you life's greatest gift, which is time when mastered.

Deciding who you're going to be in a relationship with for the long run is one of the most important decisions you'll ever make in your life. This is why it should never be taken lightly. There is no need to rush into making these decisions. Being with the right person can do wonders for your peace of mind. It can give a deeper meaning to life and make it more exciting.

Being with the wrong person can be devastating. It can make you want to give up on any ambition you've ever had for yourself. I hope this chapter challenged you to think deeply about your situation. Always remember you are in charge of your life. The moment you begin making decisions out of wisdom is when your life begins to flow smoothly.

CHAPTER FIVE

YOU DESERVE TO BE LOVED

A shley grew up as an only child. Her mother was a principal for a middle school, while her father was a truck driver. Ever since she could remember, she yearned for love from her parents. When her mother would cook meals on Sundays, Ashley always wanted to help. Since her mother was particular about how the food was cooked, she insisted that she wait for dinner out of the kitchen each time.

Ashley was close to her father too, but never saw him much growing up because of work. Not getting the love she wanted from her parents led to a seed of feeling unworthy being planted. When Ashley entered high school, she was eager to get the love she craved. She would do anything with a man to be with them, even if it meant sabotaging her reputation. While her intentions were pure, she quickly became labeled as *fast*. Since it was easy for any man to get with her, no one ever took her seriously. Years later, when she became an adult, Ashley finally found someone that she loved. Unfortunately, the love was not mutual, and eventually, he ended the relationship.

These stories are more common than you think. So many of our desires are strong because of what wasn't fulfilled when we were younger. We then do whatever we can to fulfill these needs. Even if it means going against our values which leads to regret.

Over the years, I've been able to observe successful and unsuccessful relationships. Sometimes in life, the people you love may not love you back, which can cause you to feel drained. It's important to remember that if you're not acknowledged by one person, there are plenty of others who would value you. While some people may cause you pain, even more, will add joy. Letting go of what hurts creates the space for something wonderful to come into your life. No matter what you've been through, you are worthy. We sometimes think we don't deserve love because of past experiences. This causes us to dwell on mistakes we have made and perhaps relive them. We are not our past.

The woman reading these pages has something incredible to offer. She must first acknowledge that the love she desperately wants to give she also deserves. Join personal development seminars and workshops as a chance to interact with people more. Surround yourself with people who love themselves so that it influences you. As Jim Rohn said, " For things to change, YOU have to change. For things to get better, YOU have to get better. For things to improve, YOU have to improve. When YOU grow, EVERYTHING in your life grows with you."

The Girl In A Wheelchair

Hannah was born with a disease called Spinal Muscular Atrophy. This is a genetic disease that affects the central nervous system, peripheral nervous system, and voluntary muscle movement. Her parents were immediately told that she wouldn't make it to her fifth birthday. So, Hannah grew up not ever knowing how long she was going to live. Her childhood was consumed with doctor appointments. Each one would give a different estimate of how much time she had left. Acknowledging this at such a young age inspired her to live to the fullest while she was here.

Hannah was known as 'The girl in a wheelchair' as a child, and this would often upset her. It wasn't until she got older that her perspective changed. She realized that the wheelchair was actually an asset and not a burden. If she didn't have this special chair on wheels, it would have made it much more difficult to get around. She began to love herself and the wheelchair for what it did for her. While her self esteem grew from the love she had for herself, she was having difficulty finding love in relationships.

Hannah would go out on dates, but nothing ever lasted because of her disability. She still didn't know how long she would live, if she could have children, and what would happen in the years to come. While she learned to accept her unknown future, the guys she met never could. So, Hannah made up her mind that she would always be single. There was no use in trying and getting her hopes up anymore.

After graduating college, she and her best friend moved to California. A few months later, they began attending a church. One day after service, a man approached her and immediately began conversing with her. His name was Joshua. As he was asking questions, Hannah was waiting for the common question of "Why are you in a wheelchair?" but to her surprise, it never came. This was the first time that someone was hitting on her without acknowledging her wheelchair. Joshua seemed to be so into the conversation that he never brought it up.

Eventually, he gave her his name and number, and they went on with their day. They began texting, and Hannah could immediately tell that he liked her, but no matter what, she refused to date because of past experiences. She was still afraid of someone else telling her they couldn't see a future with her because of her chair.

Hannah would often take days and sometimes weeks to respond. Nevertheless, Joshua was patient and would resume texting once he got her response. He would ask her out on dates, and every time Hannah would find a way out of it. It took about three months for her to finally agree, but even then, she had her guard up. She couldn't picture anyone wanting to spend their life with someone who wasn't independent.

They remained friends for close to a year. Around this time, her best friend that she moved to California with, got married and moved back to Utah. Not able to support herself on her own, she was thinking of moving back as well. When she told Joshua this, he immediately offered her a place to stay with his family. It wasn't until that night he confessed his desire to be with her. While she was still hesitant, she decided to take a chance and be with him. What made this man stand out to Hannah so much was that he never made her feel insecure about her disability. Whenever they spoke, he was always present with each moment.

A few weeks went by, and it finally happened; Hannah had fallen in love. He eventually proposed to her, and it was the greatest day of their lives. Joshua helps her shower, get dressed, and into bed every night. While they do have conversations about kids, he lets it be known that he wants her more than them.

I hope this story touched you and reminded you of what's possible in your life. No matter your reasons for why you think no one would want to be with you. There is always someone willing to appreciate who you are. We have to learn to keep the door open to love. Having a bad experience is not a reason to close it completely. The right person can add to your life and make it more joyful when you're willing to let them in. Keep the door open to love, and never stop loving yourself.

CHAPTER SIX

ONLY WHEN
THEY LOSE YOU

J ennifer was out at a bar one night with her girls. They were celebrating 10 years of being in a sorority together. Everyone was drinking and having an amazing time. Sitting one table away, Brian noticed she was the only one of her friends with no ring on her finger. He used this opportunity to buy her a drink and heads over.

They struck up a conversation and hit it off immediately. It turned out they grew up in the same neighborhood. They began dating, and things got serious quickly. Soon Jennifer started to notice that Brian was out late every night. Regardless of if she was able to go too, it never slowed him down.

Jennifer did not think anything about it until friends brought it to her attention. Some of them were telling her that they would see him approaching other women. When Jennifer confronted Brian, he initially denied it. But eventually, he told her the truth and promised to not let it happen again.

For a few months, everything seemed to be better. Then one night, after an argument, Brian went back to his old ways. Jennifer continued to insist he change and even left him many times. Each time Brian would make enough changes to get her back, then slowly return to old habits. This kept going on until, finally, she gave up. Eventually, she accepted his ways and stopped trying anymore. She spent the rest of her life miserable but pretended she was happy.

Many times in life, you may meet people that take you for granted. It can cause you to feel pain when you've done all that you can do. These same people will attempt to enter into your life again very often when you've made a positive impact. It's important to remember that it is always your choice if you want them back in your life. Just because time has moved forward, and you've changed, it doesn't mean that the person you were with changed as well.

Losing someone is hard. It's even more difficult when you've made a great impression. This not only applies to intimate relationships. It's applicable to your friendships as well. Everyone in your space has to show appreciation just as you do. Relationships thrive and come alive when built on gratitude. I've had plenty of friends who have been in relationships with narcissistic individuals. These people are manipulators and believe the world revolves around them. They will do anything in their power to control you and the relationship.

For instance, one day, a friend of mine began to publicly date a guy she met. After seeing a picture of them on my social media feed, I decided to call and congratulate her. I was expecting her to be excited since she had not been in a relationship for years. However, when I spoke to her, that was not the case.

She had only been official for a few hours and was already stressed out. I discovered that her new man immediately became insecure. He began accusing her of lying, blowing up her phone with multiple messages at a time. She kept engaging in his manipulation until I told her to stop responding. Silence can be the best medicine for out-of-control behavior. I told her that eventually, he would apologize, and it would be up to her whether she accepted and moved forward. She chose to end the relationship once she got the call from him.

Keeping these types of people in your life does a disservice to you and them. No one will ever evolve without learning lessons. While the painful ones are usually avoided, they often provide the most growth. When you decide to move forward with your life, it motivates change. This action alone could make them a better partner for their next relationship.

This is a lesson that makes life easier when understood. So many people across the globe have wasted time in relationships from not grasping it sooner. They then feel it may be too late to get involved with anyone else. Each story is different. There are people who have successfully changed when given the chance.

They searched for help and made a transformation in their life. The thought of losing someone can inspire you in many ways.

Unfortunately, there are also others who make temporary changes. These people are only focused on getting you back into their space. They will use every tactic to make it appear that they are a different person. Once you let your guard down, you then find yourself in familiar territory, not appreciated and unfulfilled and asking the questions you've asked yourself before; "Why am I still in this? Why is this happening to me?"

As simple as it sounds, the only way to stop running in circles is to stop running. Take your mind off autopilot. Give yourself an opportunity to observe the red flags. Then be prepared to make subtractions in your life for good. No looking back. Each time you do, you are only losing time that could be spent with someone worth it. You will know if someone has changed for the better. Bad behavior cannot be hidden for long.

The love for yourself has to drive you to make those tough decisions. It has to override the fear of temporarily being alone. When doubts come to your mind on whether you should leave, think about the pain you've already experienced in the relationship. Remind yourself that nothing will ever change until you do.

CHAPTER SEVEN

TAKING RESPONSIBILITY

A dam was the first man created. Shortly thereafter, God realized it was not good for man to be alone. Seeing that he needed a helper, God created a woman for him. Her name was Eve.

Everything was peaceful at this time. They both were living in paradise without a worry in the world. Then one day, a serpent manipulated Eve into eating from the forbidden tree. This tree was the only one that they were told to not eat from. She then convinced Adam to do the same. When God found out about this,

Adam quickly blamed Eve. Then in response, Eve immediately blamed the serpent. I would not be surprised if the serpent tried to blame the tree. This may perhaps be the beginning of not taking responsibility.

No matter your beliefs, you are probably familiar with that story. I watched an interview with comedian Bill Burr recently that caught my attention. He mentioned that as adults, we are our own parents. That statement could not be any more true, especially when you have your own place. There is no one telling you how late you should be awake, what foods you should eat, how to budget your money. It is all up to you. You are with yourself 24 hours a day. The adult supervision you now have comes from you looking after yourself.

I'm sure you have heard of the concept of taking responsibility. This chapter was written to make sure you actually do it. Not only for the areas you feel comfortable doing it, but with everything. Blaming is a toxic habit. It is also one of the easiest things you can do. It's a convenient way to let yourself off the hook. Once you begin blaming others for one part of your life, you will soon do the same for others. Not having control leads to feeling powerless.

The key to feeling empowered comes from ownership. Do you remember how you felt when you first purchased something that was yours? Your first car, pet, or even your own home? I'm sure you felt a sense of accomplishment. You then knew moving forward that you would be responsible for taking care of that purchase. That means that when the car gets dirty, you need to clean it. When your pet needs to be taken to the vet, you make time to do it. If something needs to be fixed at home, you take care of it. Complaining is never the solution to your problems. Once you're done, you still have the same problems to deal with. Deliberate action will always be the key. Here's a story of a woman who despite her deplorable upbringing, committed herself to take control of her life.

Her name is Dawn Watson. I learned about her from watching Tony Robbins's documentary *I Am Not Your Guru*. Tony was searching for someone who was genuinely suicidal. He was meticulous in his search as he didn't want anyone who just wanted attention.

Finally, he came across a woman by the name of Dawn. She was calm at first but then began to open up about her pain. Through tears, she explained how she was raised in a religious cult called The Children Of God. In this cult, she was taught to have sex with people to please God. This little girl grew up seeing her whole family abused. Everyone around her, including herself, was depressed. Despite this upbringing, she still managed to have another vision of God. She knew that this was not the way to live life.

After sharing her story, she was embraced by everyone in the room. Tony even offered to put her through training so that she could help others who went through similar experiences. You can learn more about her story in her book *My Journey Back Home.* Dawn went through unimaginable pain. Something that many of us have never even heard of. She couldn't help that she went through such an experience. However, she took full responsibility for how she was going to live the rest of her life.

Not all of us were fortunate enough to have the most loving parents. We all come from different backgrounds and cultures. Some of us were reared with love as children. Others were abused and many times neglected. Nevertheless, we all have the same responsibility when we become adults. How we choose to live our lives will be up to us.

If someone you loved left you recently, it is not an excuse for bad behavior or poor habits. This is not something I write lightly. I'm aware of the pain that is felt when someone leaves. But I also understand that they are not responsible for how you live your life. You are the only one. You are grown. You can no longer blame anything outside yourself for your actions. The woman reading these pages has to begin taking action. Anything she is unsatisfied with in her life needs to change now. If she's not in a healthy relationship, that needs to change.

If you're unhappy with your career, changes need to be made. If you're living in an unsafe neighborhood, that needs to change. Keep in mind that this is not something that you should do once in a while. This needs to become a daily habit of how you're going to live. For the rest of your life, you will be overcoming obstacles.

You conquer them much faster when you take responsibility. You

can either spend energy blaming others or spend that same energy

solving your issues. The choice will ultimately be up to you.

CHAPTER EIGHT

THE STRENGTH
OF A WOMAN

"Look what you made me do, Angie. You made me shoot you." These are the words that came out of her boyfriend's mouth. Angela's relationship with her man started off wonderful, as most do. They had known one another for 20 years. She claimed that he was a good person. Shortly after his mom died was when he started to change. It began as verbal abuse, then eventually, he became combative. He ended up purchasing a machete and a shotgun.

One day after a heated argument, Angela asked her boyfriend to leave the house. As she walked over to the door to lead him out, he grabbed her by the hood of her sweatshirt, threw her down to the ground, and began choking her. If it wasn't for her oldest son hearing her scream, she might have been choked to death. They broke up for a while, but Angela made the mistake of getting back with him.

Things did not change. It was the same scenario of her having an argument with her boyfriend but this time it escalated to something much worse than she could imagine. While Angela was in the bathtub, her boyfriend came in and shot her. She could only remember the last two gunshots. She looked up at him, and he said, "Look what you made me do, Angie. You made me shoot you." Strangely enough, he ended up calling 911 for her.

Angela didn't realize it at the time, but she became paralyzed from the shooting. Paramedics arrived on-site and loaded her into the ambulance. In the midst of the pain and tears that were coming down her cheeks, Angela's focus was not on herself. She said to the female paramedic, "Please don't let me die. I have four kids to raise."

The paramedics didn't let her die. Angela survived nine gunshots and never cried once about being paralyzed. She does public speaking about gun violence, domestic violence, and mental health any chance she gets.

One of the reasons toxic relationships last for so long is because of a fear that you'll never meet someone who will love and accept you. You start to believe the lies that have been told over the years. You then go on pretending to be happy, but you know you are not. The only way to get what you deserve is to let go of what hurts you.

There's a man or woman for everyone who's willing to trust that their arrival will come. The sooner you let go, the sooner you will receive. As Tony Robbins said, "If you question something long enough, you'll begin to doubt it."

Think about all of the lies you may have been told up to this point. Grab a pencil and write each of them down. The next thing I want you to do is to begin questioning them. Is this true? Or was this just a form of manipulation? Anything that was meant to damage you, let it go now. Replace the lies with words of empowerment. I am worthy. I am strong. I am beautiful. I deserve to be appreciated. I have so much to offer. Begin approaching your life with more confidence. This next story is an example of a woman who made a transformative decision just in time.

Jane met her future boyfriend when he moved next door to her. They started off as friends, and then some time afterward, he moved in with her. They would do everything together: go out to parties, dance every night, and drink a lot.

One evening as they were out with friends drinking, his ex happened to stop by, and they kissed in front of Jane. Upset by this, she stormed off and locked herself in their car. Her boyfriend came and punched his fist through the passenger window, hitting her in the head. When one of his friends saw this, they insisted they drive her home. Jane was in disbelief of what happened that night. Things had never gotten so out of hand.

The following day he was full of guilt and promised not to drink again. She believed him, and things went well for a while but soon got progressively worse. One night as she was pregnant, he punched her in the stomach. Thankfully she did not lose the baby. The next day he apologized as usual and was forgiven again.

Years later, they ended up staying with his parents, which Jane thought would be better for all of them. Only to find out that the father had a drinking problem as well, which influenced him even more. It wasn't until an incident that happened with her babies that she knew she had to leave.

Jane had been out running errands and came back home to check on her kids. She went upstairs and found a shirt wrapped around her infant's head with the shirt shoved in the baby's mouth. Apparently, the baby had been crying, and this was his way of not having to hear it.

That night when the boyfriend and his parents left the house and went to visit family members, she developed the courage to call Domestic Violence and get help. Jane's life began to change for the better after that phone call. She was embraced with open arms as she was able to arrive at their facility safely. A few years later, she met a man that not only loved her but loved her kids just as much. She feels that her life is now complete, and she finally has the family she always wanted.

The late Maya Angelou said, "When someone shows you who they are, believe them the first time. They know themselves more than you ever could know them." None of us are perfect. Everyone will have their moments of saying something or responding out of character. However, abuse should never be ignored.

You have the same courage and strength that these women had. It's your choice whether you use it or not. If you ever find yourself feeling weak, and that happens to us all, I want you to remember these women's stories. It's a reminder that there is a light at the end of the tunnel when you begin to search for it. As with any muscle, you become stronger with repetition. Just like your quads grow stronger with each squat, so do you emotionally when you remove yourself from hurtful situations. Promise yourself today to no longer tolerate abusive behavior from anyone.

CHAPTER NINE

ALWAYS BE YOU

L ife can be challenging. I'm sure you have had experiences that were not the most pleasant. We all have. You may have done nothing to deserve it, and yet it happened to you. There's nothing that can be said to erase these painful memories. There are only solutions to prevent you from reliving them as much, like giving it a different meaning as you read in the previous chapters, but also learning about others who went through similar experiences and came out victorious.

You, too, can do the same. Each of us is a story waiting to be told. You did not go through your pain, only for you to bury it deep down inside. It's an opportunity to share it with someone who may be going through it now.

I remember meeting a woman years ago confiding in me about a breakup. She was devastated and promised herself not to love again. She wanted to be a completely different person and treat people as bad as she had been treated. I told her while making changes for the better is wisdom; changing who you are for the worse is never the answer.

Sometimes we can get caught up in our feelings and make irrational decisions. Pain is the teacher that will be with you for the rest of your life. No one will escape their lessons no matter how hard they try to. It would be foolish to think otherwise. If we all made poor changes, whenever we felt pain, there would be no hope in the world. We all have choices on how to respond to each experience.

Some people choose to let pain destroy their lives. They allow it to consume them, causing them to feel bitter. It has changed how they once viewed the world. These people are miserable and want everyone around them to feel the same. Others will choose to let pain transform their lives. These are the people who will use it to reach new levels mentally. They believe that everything is happening for their good. No matter the adversity, they refuse to be changed negatively. They know that more people will appreciate them rather than take advantage.

All the good you have to offer should never change. No matter who took it for granted, there are always people who would embrace it. Give these people a chance. Search relentlessly until you find them. It's worth it. I'm going to end this chapter with words I wrote years ago that are still true to this day.

As each of us goes through our chapters in life, we are all faced with unique challenges. Circumstances may not always be so kind. Obstacles and people can greatly affect how we perceive this world. While we should learn valuable lessons from each experience life has to offer us, we must remember to stay true to our essence. Allow it all to cultivate us into an even more remarkable person. Let each experience inspire us to gain access to the unbelievable strength we've had all along. Be not fearful of vulnerability if we feel that our love was taken for granted with one person, but rather rest assured knowing that all we put into this world we shall receive back abundantly, even if it's not with the person we gave so openly to. No matter wherever you find yourself in life, remember to always be you.

AFTERWORD

L ife is precious. Sometimes when we go through the day, we seem to forget that statement. We can get caught up in our feelings and make situations more dramatic, not realizing that they are often not as serious as we made them out to be.

I recently read about a 24-year-old woman in India who wanted to end her life after a breakup. She went to the Yamuna Canal to jump into the water but changed her mind at the last minute. The woman then decided to Google less painful ways to commit suicide. While searching for ways to end her life, she came across suicide helpline numbers which inspired her to call and get help. She ended up speaking to the deputy inspector of police, who thankfully convinced her to come to his office. The woman was then sent to counseling, where she successfully got more of the help she needed.

Sometimes in life, you may feel like your world is ending. Certain situations can influence you to lose faith. No matter what you're facing, you have the ability to persevere. The pain you experience is always only for a moment.

Instead of dwelling on what hurts you, seek help from people that can guide you. There is never a reason to end your life. Whenever those thoughts attempt to enter your mind, remind yourself of the people who love you, the people who would forever be devastated by your loss. I encourage you to even think about the people you would never meet. The ones who went through similar experiences and needed to hear your story for encouragement. We all need one another in a positive way.

This book was written to be read whenever your mind forgets the truth. Self-love immediately enhances your value. All of your decisions throughout the day should come from this foundation. You will find yourself feeling more confident when you make this a priority.

Living this way helps you become a loving individual. You will now have more to give others because you're giving to yourself first. Attempting to love someone while neglecting your needs never leads to a desired outcome. You will always feel drained when you do. We have to be able to rely on ourselves for authentic self-love. Knowing what's acceptable and unacceptable will mean everything to your peace of mind.

I would like to end this book with one of my favorite quotes from Lance Armstrong. "Pain is temporary. It may last a minute, or an hour, or a day, or a year, but eventually, it will subside, and something else will take its place. If I quit, however, it lasts forever."

ACKNOWLEDGMENTS

This book is filled with stories shared with me by friends and people I've met personally. I'm deeply grateful and acknowledge your contributions. There are also people I have not met personally; for this reason, many names have been changed to protect their privacy. In addition to hearing stories and doing research online, I don't always remember the exact source of the story. What I do remember is that it is something that could motivate the reader. I thank you all for being an example to every woman who reads this book and feels inspired. The ones who were at a loss of hope but felt uplifted from hearing your story. Thank you for not giving up when it felt easy to do so. I am also grateful to my family and everyone who has supported me throughout my journey.

I need your help. If you enjoyed this book, please leave a rating and review on Amazon. My goal is to uplift as many women as possible. Your ratings help spread the word tremendously. Thanks with gratitude!

ABOUT THE AUTHOR

Alexander McEwen is an actor and author of two books in the field of self-development. This is his second book to be released with Dreamworld Believe In Yourself Again being his first. Alexander always finds ways to inspire people to live their dreams while he lives his.

INSTAGRAM: TheAlexanderMcEwen

TWITTER : Alexander McEwen

FACEBOOK: www.facebook.com/Alexander McEwen

Made in the USA
Las Vegas, NV
16 November 2022

59507448R00052